REALLY—
IT'S NOT YOU,
IT'S ME...

REALLY—
IT'S NOT YOU,
IT'S ME...

CARTOONS ABOUT LOVE,
SEX AND RELATIONSHIPS
BY ANDREW WELDON

Riverhead Books
New York

THE BERKLEY PUBLISHING GROUP
Published by the Penguin Group
Penguin Group (USA) Inc.
375 Hudson Street, New York, New York 10014, USA
Penguin Group (Canada), 90 Eglinton Avenue East, Suite 700, Toronto, Ontario M4P 2Y3,
Canada (a division of Pearson Penguin Canada Inc.)
Penguin Books Ltd., 80 Strand, London WC2R 0RL, England
Penguin Group Ireland, 25 St. Stephen's Green, Dublin 2, Ireland
(a division of Penguin Books Ltd.)
Penguin Group (Australia), 250 Camberwell Road, Camberwell, Victoria 3124, Australia
(a division of Pearson Australia Group Pty. Ltd.)
Penguin Books India Pvt. Ltd., 11 Community Centre, Panchsheel Park,
New Delhi—110 017, India
Penguin Group (NZ), Cnr. Airborne and Rosedale Roads, Albany, Auckland 1310, New Zealand
(a division of Pearson New Zealand Ltd.)
Penguin Books (South Africa) (Pty.) Ltd., 24 Sturdee Avenue, Rosebank, Johannesburg 2196,
South Africa

Penguin Books Ltd., Registered Offices: 80 Strand, London WC2R 0RL, England

REALLY—IT'S NOT YOU, IT'S ME

The cartoons in this collection originally appeared in *I'm So Sorry Little Man, I Thought You Were
a Hand-Puppet*, published by Allen & Unwin, Australia, 2002
First Riverhead trade paperback edition: June 2006
Riverhead trade paperback ISBN: 1-59448-197-0

An application to register this book for cataloging has been submitted to the Library of Congress.

Many thanks to Erica Wagner and Jake Morrissey

PRINTED IN THE UNITED STATES OF AMERICA

10   9   8   7   6   5   4   3   2   1

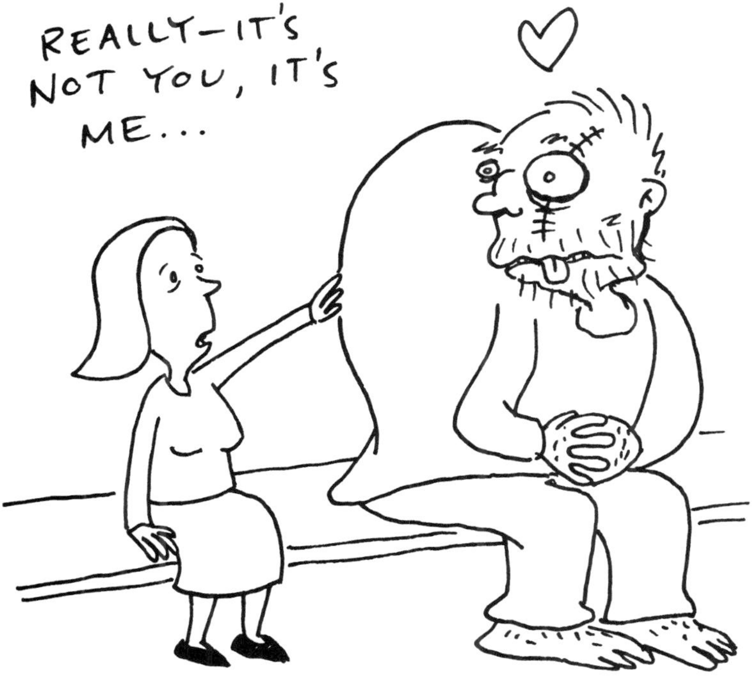
REALLY—IT'S NOT YOU, IT'S ME...

CONTEMPORARY ROMANCE

WHEN YOU SAY YOU
DON'T LOVE ME ANYMORE
IT MAKES ME THINK
YOU DON'T LOVE ME
ANYMORE.

...STOCK MARKETS ARE DOWN,
THE YEN IS DOWN,
GOLD IS DOWN.
AND I HAVEN'T
BEEN 100%
SINCE JENNY
LEFT...

SAFE SEX

SAFE:	SAFER:	SAFEST:
MONOGAMY	MAHOGANY	MAHOGANY MONOGAMY

aweldon.

FREUD AT HOME.

FOR ALAN LOVING WAS MORE
IMPORTANT THAN BEING LOVED.

SHE'S GOT A HUGE VOCABULARY — I HAVE TO KEEP A DICTIONARY BY THE BED TO TELL IF SHE'S HAVING AN ORGASM OR TELLING ME OFF.
a weldon.

aweldon

The Free Market Brady Bunch.

COW.

HIP
COW.

REALLY
HIP
COW.

aweldon.

TERMINALLY-ILL
ADVERTISING
EXECUTIVE.

THAT'S MY BEEPER – IT GOES OFF AT 4.15 EVERY DAY TO REMIND ME TO REVEL IN THE GLORY OF LIFE...
BEEP
BEEP
BEEP
aWeldon

MOBILE PHONES GET **TOO** SMALL.

TECHNOLOGY FOR JADED AUDIENCES.

EASILY SATISFIED.

JACKSON   POLLOCK GOES TO THE TOILET.

GREAT ARTS LEADERS # 3

1469 – GIOVANNI CERANELLI
INVENTS ABSTRACT EXPRESSIONISM
(500 YEARS TOO EARLY)

RICH KIDS PLAY 'PIN THE TAIL ON THE RENOIR'

ARCHITECTS' CHILDREN.

THE 'NAUGHTY' KIDS GET THEIR REVENGE

THINGS NOT TO SAY TO YOUR BANK MANAGER:

THANKS SO MUCH FOR THE LOAN – I DON'T KNOW HOW I'LL EVER REPAY YOU...

"YEAH, THE NEW JOB'S OK. LOTS OF POLITICS THOUGH."

MY WORKPLACE IS
VERY PROGRESSIVE.
— I'M OFF ON THREE DAYS
PAID CONCEPTION
LEAVE.

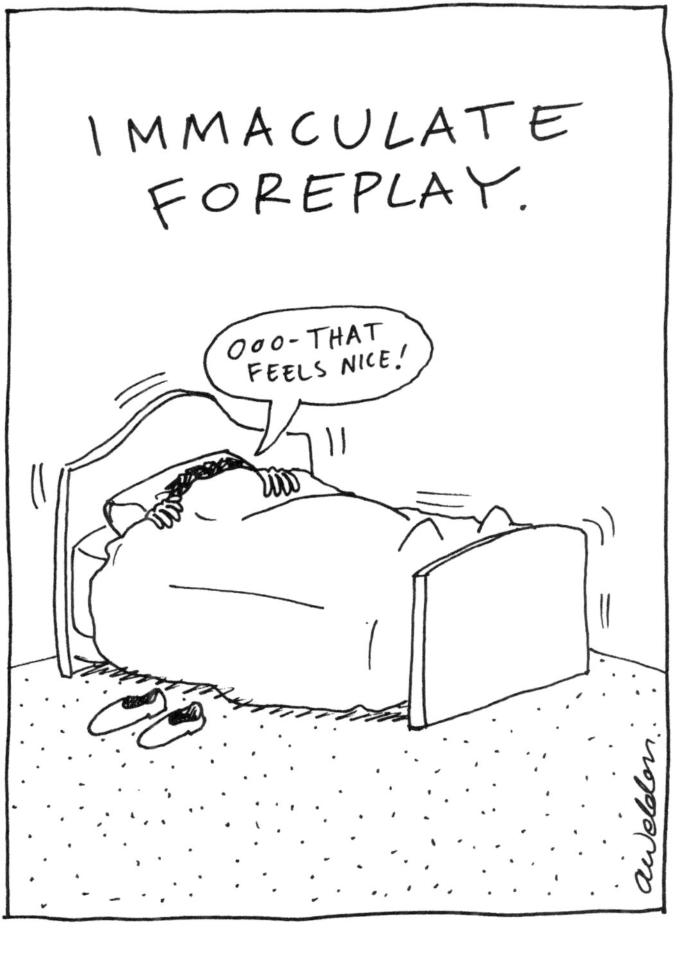
IMMACULATE FOREPLAY.
OOO-THAT FEELS NICE!

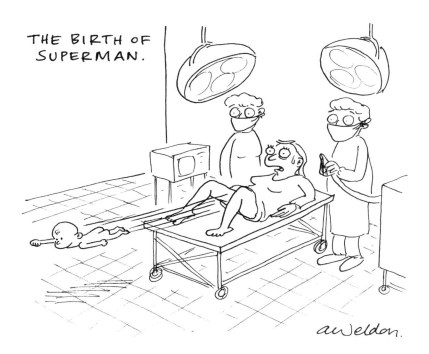

THE BIRTH OF SUPERMAN.

aWeldon.

THE BIRTHMARK
WOULDN'T HAVE
BEEN THAT BAD
- BUT HER NAME
WAS JANET.

First Day of School.

REMEMBER WHAT I TOLD YOU —
DON'T EAT ALL YOUR LUNCH AT
PLAYTIME, IF YOU HAVE TO GO TO
THE TOILET PUT YOUR HAND UP
AND ASK THE TEACHER, DON'T
TALK TO STRANGERS, DON'T
PICK YOUR NOSE, DON'T HAVE
SEX WITHOUT
A CONDOM,
AND DON'T
SHARE NEEDLES.

aWeldon.

FIRST TIME OPEN HEART SURGERY.

BEFORE
THE
PARTY...

TRICKS WITH KITTENS #1

·

JOIN THE DOT